Design and Make
PICTURE
FRAMES

Susie Hodge

FRANKLIN WATTS
LONDON•SYDNEY

Contents

Framing pictures

This book shows you how to create your own unique picture frames, using things you can find around your home. You can make a golden frame, like one for a famous painting in a gallery, or even design a frame to display your whole family tree!

Why do we frame pictures?

Why do you think we put pictures in a frame? Think about what picture frames in your home look like. How do you think they make pictures or photos look different? Do they make the picture stand out more or is the frame a feature in itself?

The way a picture is framed and the design and material used can be as important as the picture itself. In the 15th century, artists

painted on wooden panels and built up the frames directly on the wood using a mixture of glue and chalk.

As artists began to paint on canvas instead of panels, the frame became a separate object attached to the finished painting. Frames became an expensive feature, designed not only to enhance the painting but also to show off the skills of the woodcarver and gilder.

New ideas

In the late 19th and early 20th centuries, artists began to use frames that related more to their paintings. Artists such as Vincent van Gogh and Georges Seurat often decorated their frames to match the painting. Some artists removed the frame altogether, believing that frames separated the painting from the viewer. More recent artists have explored the idea of making the frame part of the picture.

Le Chahut by Georges Seurat

Photographs

The invention of photography in 1839 meant a new type of picture to display. The Victorians loved the idea that they could have a family portrait without it costing them a fortune. These days, we have frames for all types of picture. They can be elegant, cute or funny. Whether you are making frames for yourself or as a present, think about personalising them and making them suit the picture.

Mounting and protecting

The simplest way to frame a picture is to stick, or mount, it onto coloured paper or card. When you mount a picture, choose a colour that blends well with the picture and makes it look good. Framed pictures are often mounted as well. Sometimes they are protected by glass or plastic, too. Think about whether or not you are going to mount the pictures you put in your frames and how you are going to protect them.

Be prepared

These two pages show you all the different materials and equipment you will need to make the frames in this book.

When you're making a frame:

* Keep everything you need in a large box or in a tidy corner of your room.

* Collect the materals gradually; there is no need to get everything at once.

* Never let paint or glue dry on your brushes — always wash them carefully in warm soapy water and rinse and dry them well.

Things you need

Art foam

Self-hardening clay or Plasticine

A selection of card, cardboard and paper in different sizes, colours and thicknesses

A selection of odds and ends, such as sequins, beads, newspapers, ribbon, pegs, buttons, silver foil, small mosaic tiles, natural sponge, and pasta shapes

Scraps of cloth, including felt, Binka (for embroidery) and medium-weight fabrics that don't fray easily, cotton and embroidery thread

Sticky-backed plastic, acetate

Equipment

Compasses and a set square

Paints, especially poster or acrylic paints and any metallic colours.

Double-sided tape, sticky tape and masking tape

Felt-tip pens and some pencils

Paint brushes

Craft knife, cutting board and strong ruler

PVA glue

You will need some kitchen towel for clearing up and an apron or old shirt to protect your clothing

Scissors, assorted needles

Cutting cardboard

The best way to cut smooth, straight lines for frames is to use a craft knife. If you are going to cut in this way, you must use a cutting board and a strong ruler. Most importantly, you must have an adult to assist you – never cut in this way without a grown-up to supervise you.

Start by placing your ruler on the line that you want to cut. Hold it there firmly, making sure that your fingers are well back from the edge of the ruler and well away from the knife. Cut by dragging the craft knife along the edge of the ruler, using the ruler to steady the knife and making sure that your fingers are away from the blade at all times.

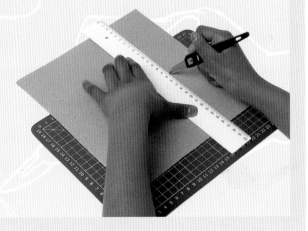

Bejewelled frame

Using sequins, beads, glitter
and other gems, make a frame
fit for a king or queen.

Look at this!

The Byzantines created magnificent
panels of gold, encrusted with priceless
jewels. This one is from the Pala D'Oro
alterpiece in St Mark's in Venice.

✱ Why do you think they liked to
use jewels and gold in their art?

Design and select

Design a glittering frame covered with jewels inspired by
Byzantine art! Think about what you will use to make the
frame and how you will decorate it. Draw a picture of your
idea and select your materials — we've used cardboard,
fake gems, beads, sequins, glitter and gold paint.

Make

1 Choose the picture you want to frame.
Use this as a guide to mark out the size
and shape of your frame and its 'window'
on a piece of cardboard. Cut out a piece
of card the same size as the frame to
make the back and set aside.

2 Cut out your frame and paint
it with metallic gold paint.
Leave it to dry for a few hours.

8

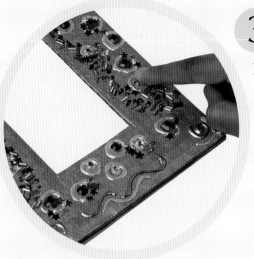

3 Arrange your gems, jewels and sequins on the frame and glue them in place when you are happy with your design. You could make a pattern or simply squeeze a little PVA glue around the frame and sprinkle the gems on. Leave to dry so the jewels are held firmly in place.

Challenge
Make a 'picture' around the frame, like a collage of sequins and glitter.

4 Measure and cut out three strips of cardboard to make 'spacers'. Glue these on the back of the frame (the card you set aside earlier) as shown, right. Spacers hold your picture in place and let you slot it in and out of the frame. Carefully glue the front of the frame onto the spacers. Don't try to glue down the fourth side — this is where your picture slots in.

5 To make a hinge stand for the frame, cut out a small rectangle of card. Fold it into three and unfold again. Glue the top third of the card onto the back of the frame, about half-way up. When the glue is dry, slot in your picture, stand the frame up and dazzle everyone!

Printed frame

Make a double frame inspired by nature to please someone special!

Look at this!

Wrapping paper and wallpaper are often printed with natural forms, such as leaves and flowers.

✱ How do you think the leaf shapes were made?

✱ How can you make the pattern repeat?

Design and select

Design a simple double frame shape, scaling its length and width according to the size of image you want to frame. Collect some leaves in different shapes and sizes, asking an adult for permission if you need to pick any of these. Think about the colours you will use to decorate this frame. Select your materials — we've used thick card for the frame, cardboard for the back of the frame, leaves and paint.

Make

1 Cut out a long rectangle of thick cardboard for the back of your frame, based on your design. With a craft knife, lightly score a vertical line down the middle on the back. Be careful not to cut all the way through. This will allow you to fold the frame like a book so that it will stand up.

2 Cut out four thin strips of cardboard about 1 cm wide to go down the sides of the frame, and two thicker strips to go along the bottom as spacer bars. Stick to the back of the frame as shown.

10

3 Cut out two pieces of thick card to make the front frames to fit on each side of the cardboard back.

4 Cover your work surface with newspaper. Paint the frame fronts a pale colour. Using darker colours, paint the underside of some of the leaves you collected. Gently press down the painted side of the leaf onto your frames to create a printed pattern.

Challenge
What else could you use for printing? How about natural sponges, lace or textured material? How could you create a stencilled design instead?

5 When the paint is dry, cut out two pieces of transparent acetate and tape them to the back of your printed frames over the windows. This will protect your pictures. Glue the printed frames onto the folding back along the spacer bars and insert your pictures.

11

Family tree

Display pictures of your whole family in one frame.

Design and select

Design a picture frame that can show your entire family at once — as many people and pets as you choose! We thought of a family tree and based our design on this. Draw a picture of your idea. Think about the materials you could use — we've used cardboard, paints and acetate.

Make

1 Copy the outline of your design onto a strong piece of cardboard to make the front of the frame and cut out carefully. Cut out another piece of card exactly the same shape for the back of the frame and set aside.

Challenge
What other designs could you use to display your whole family?

2 Use compasses to draw enough circles on the frame front for your family members. Make sure they are big enough for the photos. Ask an adult to help you cut out the circles using a craft knife or scissors. Now place the frame front on the frame back and draw round the inside of the circles, so you will know where to stick the photos.

3 Cut out your photos, place them in the right position on the frame back and stick them down using double-sided sticky tape. You can always make a photocopy of a photograph if you don't want to cut up the original picture.

Challenge
What other ways could you hold the pictures in place? Could you design a frame where the pictures slot in and out?

4 Paint the front of the frame using browns and greens and leave it to dry.

Challenge
How could you make the tree three-dimensional?

5 Stick a sheet of acetate on the back of the frame front using double-sided sticky tape. This will protect your photographs.

6 Stick the front of the frame to the back using glue or tape. Make a stand for your family tree out of a triangular piece of cardboard with an extra flap on one edge to glue down. Now your family tree is ready to display.

Art Deco frame

Make an artistic frame out of stiff card and sticky-backed plastic, using a famous design style as your inspiration.

Look at this!

Art Deco designs were inspired by many different cultures, even by the discovery in 1922 of the tomb of the ancient Egyptian Pharaoh, Tutankhamun. Art Deco used bright colours, sharp contrasts and geometric shapes to create designs.

✱ What sort of shapes have been used on this building?

Design and select

Design a frame out of shiny materials and contrasting colours. How many picture 'windows' will it have? Will the frame stand up or hang from a wall? Design your frame on paper and select your materials — we've used stiff card and metallic sticky-backed plastic.

Make

1 Copy your design onto a large piece of card and cut it out. Make an exact copy of the frame shape for the back and set aside.

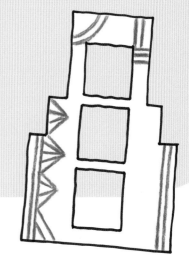

2 On the frame front, draw on your 'windows'. You could make these different shapes and sizes depending on the pictures you want to display. Ask an adult to help you cut out the windows with a craft knife.

3 To decorate your frame, cut out some sticky-backed plastic that is about 2 cm wider than the frame all the way round. Fold the sticky-backed plastic around your card frame and stick it down neatly. Carefully smooth out any air bubbles.

❊ Tip: you will find it easier to cover corners if you cut off small triangles from each corner of the plastic. Cut a cross inside each window and fold back the plastic.

Challenge
What material could you use instead of sticky-backed plastic?

4 Add detail to the frame by using shapes cut out of sticky-backed plastic in a contrasting colour. Carefully stick these shapes onto your covered frame. Cut a strip of acetate and stick this behind the windows to protect your pictures.

5 Make spacers to fit between the front and back of the frame. Glue these strips on the edges of the back. Stick your pictures in position.

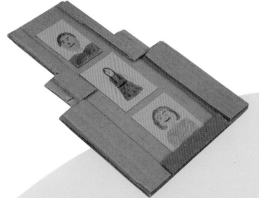

6 Glue the frame front to the back. Make a stand for your frame out of a triangle of cardboard with an extra flap to glue down.

Challenge
Investigate a design style called Art Nouveau. Design a frame based on this.

A handy peg

A peg stand can be a really handy way to display a piece of artwork or a photograph! It's so easy we've made two picture holders.

Design and select

Design a picture holder based around a simple clothes peg. Think about how you'll make the peg stand up and how you can decorate it. We've attached our peg to a helping hand. Draw a sketch of your idea. Select your materials — we used coloured card, cardboard and wooden pegs.

Make

Challenge
How could you adapt a simple idea like this to make a fridge magnet?

1 On a sheet of coloured card, draw around each of your hands. Carefully cut out the two hand shapes.

Challenge
How could you adapt this frame to have mittens or gloves? How would you decorate them?

2 Using PVA glue, fix a wooden peg to the back of each hand so that the clipping part is at the top. This will hold your picture.

3 Make a stand for your frame from a rectangle of cardboard. Score a line down one side of it. Fold along the line and stick the narrower side next to the peg. Now simply stand up the hand and clip in your photo!

Challenge
Could you build up the surface of your hands, perhaps with scrunched up paper, to make them three-dimensional?

Fishy fabric frame

A fabric frame with colourful fish on it makes a stunning border for a photograph or picture.

Design and select

Design a frame made of fabric, with appliqué pieces sewn or stuck onto it. Think about what you'll use for the fabric and what your design will look like. Draw a picture of your idea and select your materials. We've used cardboard, felt, thread, ribbons, sequins and glitter.

Make

1 Based on your drawing, cut out some shapes for your design in your chosen fabric. We've made a sea-themed frame.

Challenge
What other scene could you design for this frame? What about a wild jungle?

2 Draw your frame on some cardboard and cut it out. Cut out a piece of fabric that is big enough to cover both sides of your frame. Sew it together neatly at the edges and corners.

Challenge
How could you pad out the frame or make 3-D fish?

3 Sew or glue your sea creatures onto the covered frame. Add some thin, shiny ribbons curling upwards to look like seaweed. Use sequins and glitter for the fish eyes and air bubbles.

Challenge

How else could you make your picture look like it's underwater?

4 Stick a piece of acetate to the back of the frame front. This will add to the underwater effect. Cut out a piece of cardboard the same size as the front to make the back. Stick the front and back together leaving the top side unglued so you can slot in an image (the fabric acts like spacers).

5 Cut out a small rectangle of card to make the stand. Fold the top third of this and glue this part onto the back of the frame, in the middle. Put a picture inside your finished fabric frame that matches the theme!

Golden pasta frame

This frame resembles a heavy golden frame that you often see on antique paintings. Using simple objects you can make expensive-looking frames for all your pictures.

Look at this!

Great artists have traditionally displayed their works of art in heavy, ornate golden frames like this one.

✱ How do you think a gold frame adds to the picture?

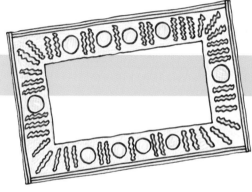

Design and select

Design a golden frame that looks expensive and striking. What sort of picture suits this frame and what could you use to decorate it? Draw a picture of your idea. Select your materials — we used cardboard, pasta shapes and gold paint.

Make

1 Mark out your frame on a piece of cardboard using a ruler and cut it out carefully. Don't forget to cut out the window, too. Cut out another piece of card the same size for the back of the frame.

2 Cut out three cardboard spacers for your frame. Carefully glue or stick these on the bottom and sides of the back of the frame. Make sure your spacers do not stick out any further than the edge of the frame.

3 Select your pasta shapes — use different sizes and shapes to give your frame lots of texture. Arrange these in a pattern on the cardboard frame and stick in position using PVA glue. Leave to dry.

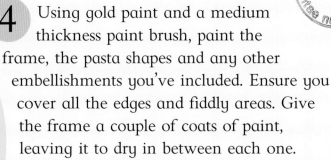

Challenge
What could you use other than pasta to create texture on the frame?

4 Using gold paint and a medium thickness paint brush, paint the frame, the pasta shapes and any other embellishments you've included. Ensure you cover all the edges and fiddly areas. Give the frame a couple of coats of paint, leaving it to dry in between each one.

Challenge
How could you make your frame a more unusual shape, like the one on page 20?

5 When the gold paint is dry, glue the front to the back of the frame and put in a picture. Make a simple hook so that the frame can be hung on a wall (see page 25).

Challenge
How could you make this frame stand up instead of hang on a wall?

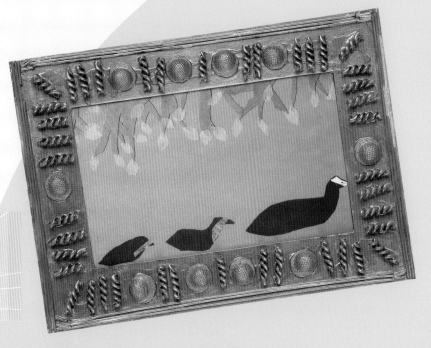

Embroidered frame

Make a padded embroidered frame.
You could use all sorts of stitches
and coloured embroidery thread or even
shiny gold thread. Try personalising
it by adding a name!

Design and select

Design an embroidered frame for your room.
Think about what you will embroider and what
colours and materials you will use. Sketch out your
idea and select your materials. We used card, wadding,
Binka fabric and gold embroidery thread.

Make

1   Draw the size and shape of your
frame on a piece of stiff card, making
sure it is big enough to fit your chosen
picture. Ask an adult to help you cut this
out carefully with scissors or a craft knife.

2   Place the frame shape onto a piece
of your fabric to work out how
much material you need. Draw lightly
around the inside and outside of the frame
with a pencil to mark the area you will
embroider. Draw another line around the
outside edge of the frame adding an extra 2 cm.

3 To cut out the window in the fabric, cut diagonally across from corner to corner to make four flaps, as shown. Then cut out the frame following the outside pencil line. Now you can begin to embroider.

4 Choose your embroidery thread and tie a knot in the end. Thread the other end through a large needle. Following your pencil marks so you know where to embroider, sew through one hole in the fabric and across and through a hole diagonally opposite. From the back, sew diagonally through the opposite side to make a little 'x'. Repeat the pattern all over the embroidery area.

5 Cut out some wadding, the exact size and shape of the frame and glue it to the frame. Now glue your embroidered fabric around the frame, folding in the flaps of material and making sure you match up the edges.

Challenge
Make a frame using ribbons sewn on the fabric instead of embroidery. How will you use the ribbons?

6 Make the back of the frame with spacers as on page 9. Fix the front of the frame to the back and make a stand – depending on whether you want the frame to hang or stand up. Put in your picture.

Far-out foam!

Make a frame out of coloured foam shapes. The foam can be bought in all colours in craft shops and is easy to work with. It can make your frames look very professional!

Design and select

Design a frame based on outer space. Think about what shapes you will cut out to decorate the frame and draw a picture of your idea. Select your materials — we used card and coloured foam.

Make

1 Draw the size and shape of your frame on a piece of coloured foam. You might want to think about what colour will suit your idea best. Draw the shape of your 'window' on the foam and cut it out.

Challenge
What other shapes could you use for the 'window' of your frame?

2 Think about the shapes you will use to decorate your frame. You might need to sketch them first. Copy your sketches onto some foam and carefully cut out the shapes.

Challenge
Make different shapes out of the foam instead – what about letters or numbers for a different theme?

3 Place your space shapes on your foam frame. Try different arrangements first before you stick them on. When you are happy with your design, stick them down with PVA glue.

4 Cut out a slightly larger foam frame in a contrasting colour. Cut a window in this and stick to the back of your decorated frame.

5 Make the back of the frame (see pages 8 and 9). Add a hook to the back using a folded piece of card with a hole cut in it. Stick the frame together, insert your picture and hang it up!

Sculptured fruit frame

A frame becomes a work of art when you sculpt tiny hand-made fruits to decorate it. Look at pictures of famous still-life paintings to get some ideas.

Design and select

Design a picture frame that is as creative and artistic as any picture that will go inside it. Consider what you will use to build up the sculpture, or relief, and draw a picture of your idea. Think about what materials you might use — we've used self-hardening clay, paints and cardboard.

Make

1 Base your frame on the drawing you made. Cut out the shape of your frame from stiff cardboard. We drew around a saucer to make the frame, but you could use compasses to make your circles instead.

2 Draw a smaller circle in the centre of your frame. Ask an adult to help you cut this out carefully using scissors or a craft knife and cutting board.

3 Using the clay, or whatever material you have chosen to make the decorations, sculpt the tiny fruit shapes. When these are dry, paint them carefully in fruit colours.

Challenge
What could you use instead of clay to make the sculpted shapes for your frame?

26

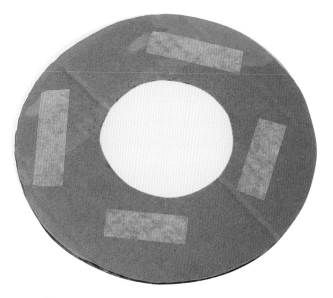

4 Paint your frame. When this is dry, stick the painted fruits around your frame with PVA glue.

Challenge
What other fruits or objects could you make?

5 Cut a sheet of acetate into a circle and stick it on the back of this frame using PVA glue or double-sided sticky tape.

6 Cut out a matching cardboard circle for the back of the frame. Create a spacer as shown using another semi-circle of card. Stick the frame together and add a hook or hinge. Now put your fabulously framed picture on display.

Challenge
Make a similar frame, but decorate with sweets.

Mosaic frame

Mosaics are very easy to make and very effective. People have made mosaics for centuries, but they are still fashionable!

Design and select

Design a picture frame using mosaic tiles. Think about the kind of mosaic you will make. Will it be a set pattern, a picture, or in a particular colour scheme? Draw a picture of your idea, then think about what materials you might use — we've used small square mosaic tiles, cardboard and grouting.

Look at this!

Spanish artist and architect Antoni Gaudi made wonderful mosaics made up of bits of glass, crockery and ceramics.

✱ What effect does the variety of materials used have?

✱ Why is it a good idea to reuse materials?

Make

1   Draw the shape of your frame on a piece of firm card. Use a ruler for the sides if necessary and measure the frame to make sure that your tiles will fit on side by side, or however you are going to arrange them.

2   Ask an adult to help you cut out your frame carefully using sharp scissors or a craft knife and cutting board. Spread PVA glue on the frame in small sections and begin to apply your tiles carefully, moving round the frame, covering one section at a time. Let the glue dry.

3 When the glue has dried, you might like to grout between the tiles to fill in any gaps. Grouting is soft, white powder that, when mixed with water, forms a kind of cement. Spread the wet grouting over the tiles and push it down between them. Wipe the excess mixture off the tiles and leave to dry.

4 Cut out the frame shape from a sheet of acetate and glue this on to the underside of the frame.

5 To make the back of the frame, cut out two pieces of card the same shape as the front and glue together. The double thickness of card will support the heavy tiles better. Attach two spacers to the sides of the frame and one to the bottom.

6 To make the frame stand up, cut out two card shapes with a diagonal edge (shown above) and glue them together. Leave a flap on either side to fold back and glue onto the frame back. Assemble all the parts and put a picture inside your mosaic frame!

Challenge
What else could you use instead of mosaic tiles? How about things you would usually recycle?

Glossary

acetate
a clear sheet of flexible material called cellulose acetate

appliqué
fabric pieces applied to other material

Binka
fabric with holes already in it for embroidery

Byzantine
from the Eastern Roman Empire, AD 395 to 1453. Its capital was Byzantium (later Constantinople and now Istanbul in Turkey)

canvas
a rough cloth made from hemp or cotton which can be painted on when stretched tightly

complement
things that go together, such as colours

embroidery
decorative needlework

geometric
designs made up of simple shapes and lines

gilder
a crafts person who specialises in covering surfaces, such as wood or plaster, in gold or gold-coloured paint or material

grouting
a white powder which mixed with water forms a kind of cement. Grouting is used to fill in cracks in walls or gaps between tiles

hinge
a joint that bends

metallic
shiny, resembling metal

relief
a picture or design that is raised up from a flat surface

repeat pattern
a pattern that is repeated across a design

spacers
strips of cardboard that are fixed between the front and back of the frame on three sides only, leaving one side open to insert a picture

stencil
a sheet of card with shapes cut out of it used to make a pattern

three-dimensional
having three dimensions, length, width and depth

transparent
see-through

wadding
soft stuffing

Further information

There are many different types of frame on display in galleries and museums, featuring both paintings and photographs. When you go, notice how the frames complement the images within them. They have either been made especially for the picture or selected for each specific picture.

Here is a selection of galleries and museums to visit:

National Gallery of Scotland
Edinburgh, Scotland
www.natgalscot.ac.uk

National Gallery of Australia,
Canberra, Australia
www.nga.gov.au

National Gallery,
London, England
www.nationalgallery.org.uk

New South Wales Art Gallery
Sydney, Australia
www.artgallery.nsw.gov.au

Tate Britain, Millbank,
London, England
www.tate.org.uk

South Australia Art Gallery
Adelaide, Australia
www.artgallery.sa.gov.au

Tate Liverpool
Liverpool, England
www.tate.org.uk/liverpool

Auckland Art Gallery.
Auckland, New Zealand
www.aucklandartgallery.govt.nz

Every effort has been made by the Publisher to ensure that these websites are suitable for children, and contain no inappropriate or offensive material. However, because of the nature of the Internet, it is impossible to guarantee that the contents of these sites will not be altered. We strongly advise that Internet access is supervised by a responsible adult.

Index

First published in 2005 by
Franklin Watts, 96 Leonard Street,
London EC2A 4XD

Franklin Watts Australia
Level 17/207 Kent Street, Sydney, NSW 2000

© Franklin Watts 2005

Editor: Rachel Tonkin; Art Director: Jonathan Hair;
Design: Matthew Lilly; Photography: Steve Shott.
Picture credits: Albright-Knox Art Gallery/Corbis: 5t. Basilica San Marco
Venice /Dagli Orti/Art Archive: 8t. Robert Harding Picture
Library/Alamy: 14t. Image Farm Inc/Alamy: 20t. Andrew Morse/Alamy:
28t. V & A Images/Alamy: 4c, 4b. Every attempt has been made to clear
copyright. Should there be any inadvertent omission please apply to the
publisher for rectification.

With thanks to Jack and Thomas Lilly D'Cruz and Peter Holmes
for the use of their drawings.

A CIP catalogue record for this book
is available from the British Library

Dewey Classification: 749'.7
ISBN 0 7496 6073 2
Printed in China